B Is for Bethlehem

A Christmas Alphabet

B Is for

Bethlehem

A Christmas Alphabet

by Isabel Wilner ✴ *illustrated by* Elisa Kleven

DUTTON CHILDREN'S BOOKS · NEW YORK

Text copyright © 1990 by Isabel Wilner
Illustrations copyright © 1990 by Elisa Kleven

Library of Congress Cataloging-in-Publication Data
Wilner, Isabel.
B is for Bethlehem: a Christmas alphabet/by Isabel Wilner;
illustrated by Elisa Kleven.—1st ed.
p.   cm.
Summary: Rhyming verses introduce the letters of the alphabet
and the events surrounding the birth of Jesus.
ISBN 0-525-44622-2
1. Children's poetry, American.   2. Christmas—Juvenile poetry.
3. Alphabet rhymes.   [1. Jesus Christ—Nativity—Poetry.
2. Christmas—Poetry.   3. Alphabet.   4. American poetry.]
I. Kleven, Elisa, ill.   II. Title
PS3573. I456725B2   1990
811'.54—dc20
[E]   89-49481 CIP AC

Published in the United States by
Dutton Children's Books,
a division of Penguin Books USA Inc.

Designer: Barbara Powderly
Printed in Hong Kong by South China Printing Co.
First Edition   10 9 8 7 6 5 4 3 2 1

**The art is mixed-media collage, using watercolor,
cut paper, and the artist's own patterns and drawings.**

For Ella Bramblett
I. W.

For my sisters, Carol and Susie,
and to the memory of our brother, Mark
E. K.

's for Augustus, emperor of Rome,
Who decreed, "To be counted, let each man go home."

B is for Bethlehem, where Joseph must go.
There he takes Mary, a long way and slow.

C is for Crowds growing larger each day
With more people, more animals filling the way.

D is for Donkey, plodding uphill and down
To carry young Mary to Bethlehem town.

E is for Evening, when darkness fills
Shallow valleys and covers low hills.

F is for Flocks—the guarded sheep
Huddled together, fast asleep.

G is for Glory, so splendid, so near.
It shines round the shepherds and fills them with fear.

H is for Heavenly Host, who sing
"Hosanna! Hosanna! Born is the King."

I is for Inn where the innkeeper said
There was not any room, not even a bed.

J is for Jesus, Immanuel holy
Cradled in straw in a stable so lowly.

K is for King who was promised of old:
Israel's ruler, by prophets foretold.

L is for Lullaby Mary would sing
To her baby, her lamb, the Messiah, the King.

M is for Manger. There Jesus lay
When awed shepherds found him asleep in the hay.

N is for Night, so quiet, so still.
Peace in the stable. Peace on the hill.

O is for Oxen that stand near the manger
Guarding and watching the new baby stranger.

P is for Presents three kings place before him
With praise and with love as they kneel to adore him.

Q is for Quest that brought them so far
Over desert and mountain, led by a star.

R is for Radiance, God's glorious light.
It brightens the stable. It lightens the night.

S is for Stable and Star, and for Story
Of animals, angels, manger, and glory.

T is for Tidings the big bells chime,
Over and over, time after time.

U is for Us. On that Christmas morn
Unto us all a child was born.

V's for Venite, the summons, O come.
Come praise him with harp and with trumpet and drum.

W's for Worship. O come and adore.
In starlight, in candlelight, glad carols soar.

X is for EXcelsis, the song angels sang.
"Gloria in excelsis" their clear voices rang.

Y is for You, for all, everywhere,
Who send those words ringing again through the air.

"...and on earth peace..."

Z is for Zeeland and Zurich and Zanzibar.
You'll be lighting the candles wherever you are.